THE ESSENTIAL COLLEC...

OPERA
GOLD

Published by:
Chester Music Limited,
8/9 Frith Street, London W1D 3JB, England.

Exclusive Distributors:
Music Sales Limited,
Distribution Centre, Newmarket Road, Bury St Edmunds, Suffolk IP33 3YB, England.
Music Sales Corporation,
257 Park Avenue South, New York, NY10010, United States of America.
Music Sales Pty Limited,
120 Rothschild Avenue, Rosebery, NSW 2018, Australia.

Order No. CH68761
ISBN 1-84449-608-2
This book © Copyright 2005 by Chester Music.

Arranging and engraving supplied by Camden Music.

Printed in the United Kingdom.

Your Guarantee of Quality:
As publishers, we strive to produce every book to the highest commercial standards.
The music has been freshly engraved and carefully designed to minimise
awkward page turns to make playing from it a real pleasure.
Particular care has been given to specifying acid-free, neutral-sized
paper made from pulps which have not been elemental chlorine bleached.
This pulp is from farmed sustainable forests and was produced
with special regard for the environment.
Throughout, the printing and binding have been planned to ensure a sturdy,
attractive publication which should give years of enjoyment.
If your copy fails to meet our high standards, please inform us and we will gladly replace it.

www.musicsales.com

CHESTER MUSIC
part of the Music Sales Group
London/New York/Paris/Sydney/Copenhagen/Berlin/Madrid/Tokyo

Art Thou Troubled?

(from 'Rodelinda')

Composed by George Frideric Handel

Au Fond Du Temple Saint

(Duet from 'The Pearl Fishers')

Composed by Georges Bizet

Arranged by Quentin Thomas

The Barber Of Seville (Overture)

(from 'The Barber Of Seville')

Composed by Gioacchino Rossini

Arranged by Quentin Thomas

Bridal Chorus
(from 'Lohengrin')

Composed by Richard Wagner

Con moto moderato

Barcarolle
(from 'The Tales Of Hoffmann')

Composed by Jacques Offenbach

pp *bien marque le chant*

simile

Chorus Of The Hebrew Slaves: Va, Pensiero

(from 'Nabucco')

Composed by Giuseppe Verdi

Casta Diva
(from 'Norma')

Composed by Vincenzo Bellini

Arranged by Simon Lesley

Dance Of The Hours
(from 'La Gioconda')

Composed by Amilcare Ponchielli

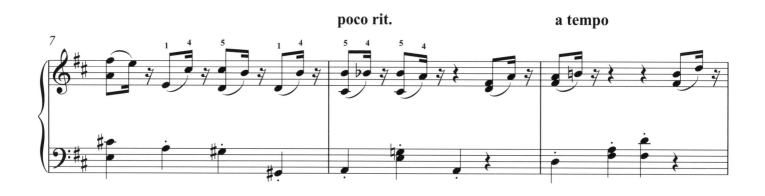

Der Vogelfänger Bin Ich Ja
(from 'The Magic Flute')

Composed by Wolfgang Amadeus Mozart

Arranged by Jack Long

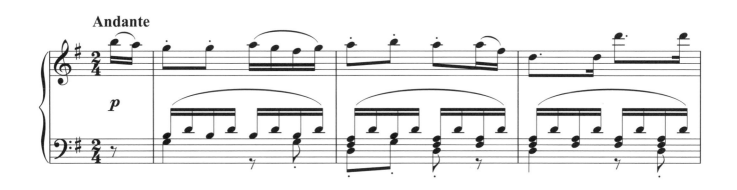

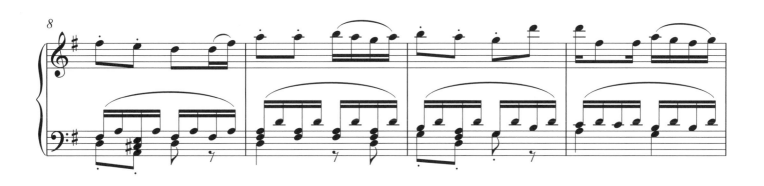

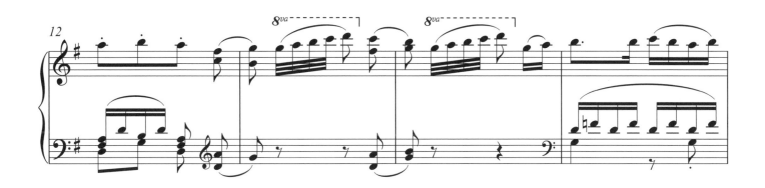

Entr'acte
(from 'Rosamunde')

Composed by Franz Peter Schubert

Andantino

Flower Duet

(from 'Lakmé')

Composed by Leo Delibes

Arranged by Jack Long

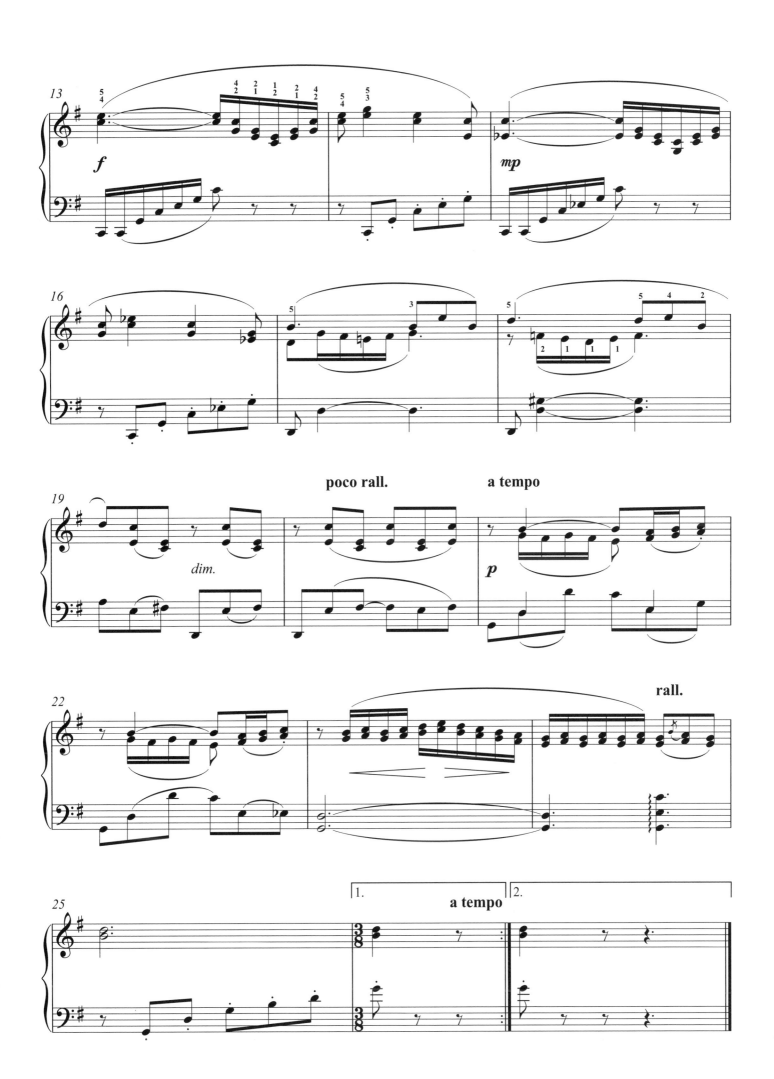

Grand March

(from 'Aida')

Composed by Giuseppe Verdi

Habañera: L'amour Est Un Oiseau Rebelle

(from 'Carmen')

Composed by Georges Bizet

Arranged by Jerry Lanning

41

Lascia Ch'io Pianga
(from 'Rinaldo')

Composed by George Frideric Handel

La Ci Darem La Mano
(from 'Don Giovanni')

Composed by Wolfgang Amadeus Mozart

Arranged by Jack Long

La Donna È Mobile

(from 'Rigoletto')

Composed by Giuseppe Verdi

Arranged by Jerry Lanning

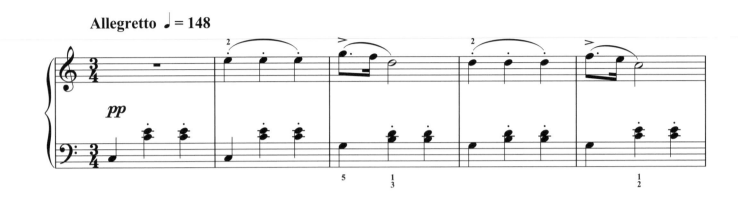

Largo: Ombra Mai Fu

(from 'Xerxes')

Composed by George Frideric Handel

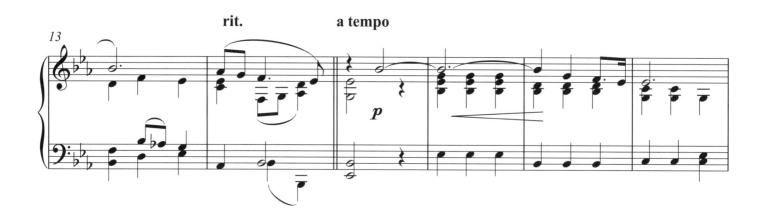

Meditation
(from 'Thaïs')

Composed by Jules Massenet

Arranged by Jerry Lanning

Minuet
(from 'Don Giovanni')

Composed by Wolfgang Amadeus Mozart

Tempo di minuetto

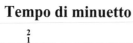

Non Più Andrai

(from 'The Marriage of Figaro')

Composed by Wolfgang Amadeus Mozart

Arranged by Jack Long

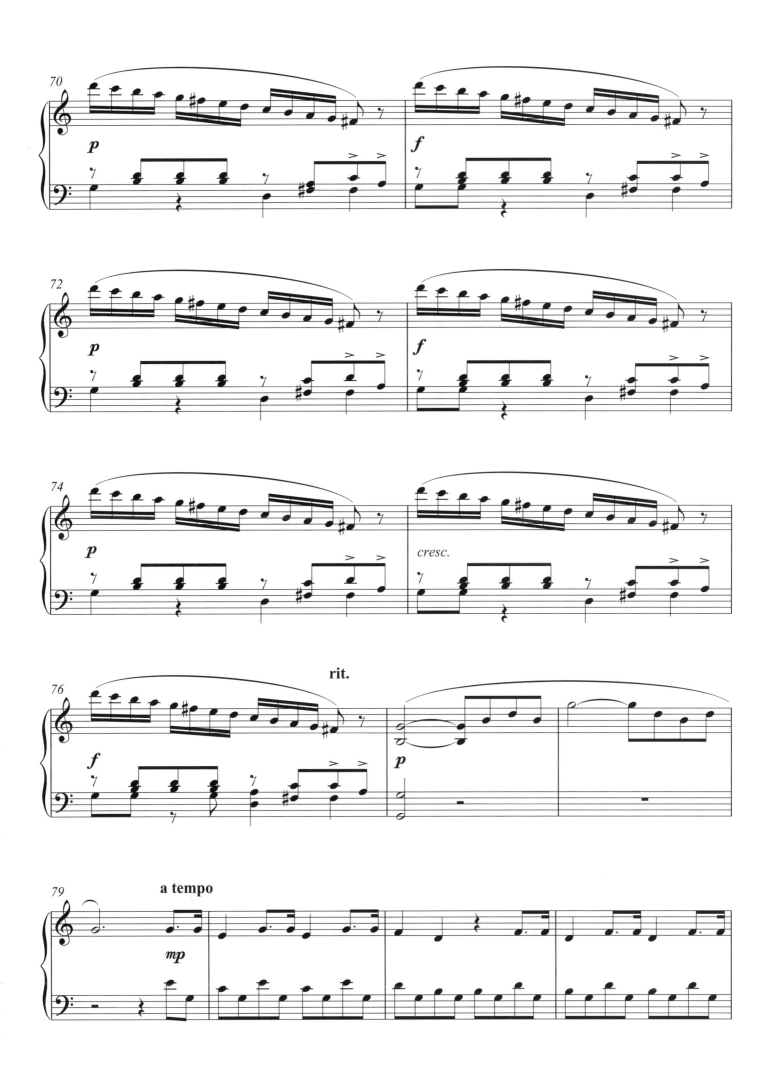

Polonaise

(from 'Eugene Onegin')

Composed by Pyotr Ilyich Tchaikovsky

Arranged by Jerry Lanning

Moderato (Tempo di polacca) ♩ = 92

Prince Gremin's Aria
(from 'Eugene Onegin')

Composed by Pyotr Ilyich Tchaikovsky

Andante sostenuto ♩ = 76

The Toreador's Song

(from 'Carmen')

Composed by Georges Bizet

Allegro molto moderato

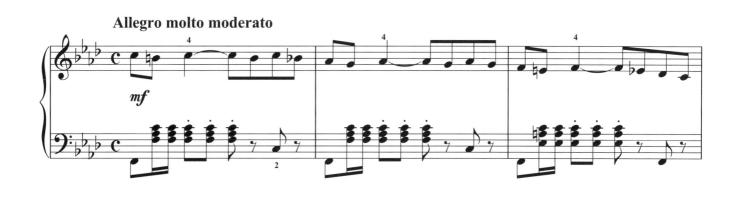

The Ride Of The Valkyries
(from 'Die Walküre')

Composed by Richard Wagner
Arranged by Jerry Lanning

Vivace ♩. = 96

Sempre Libera
(from 'La Traviata')

Composed by Giuseppe Verdi

Allegro brillante

Soave Sia Il Vento
(from 'Cosi Fan Tutte')

Composed by Wolfgang Amadeus Mozart

Arranged by Quentin Thomas

To The Evening Star
(from 'Tannhäuser')

Composed by Richard Wagner

Andante sostenuto

Voi, Che Sapete

(from 'The Marriage of Figaro')

Composed by Wolfgang Amadeus Mozart
Arranged by Jack Long

Andante con moto

'Un Certo Non So Che'
(There's One, I Know Him Not)
(from 'Arsilda, Regina di Punto')

Composed by Antonio Vivaldi
Arranged by Quentin Thomas

Con moto ed affetuoso (♩ = 69)

Waltz
(from 'Faust')

Composed by Charles François Gounod

Tempo di valse

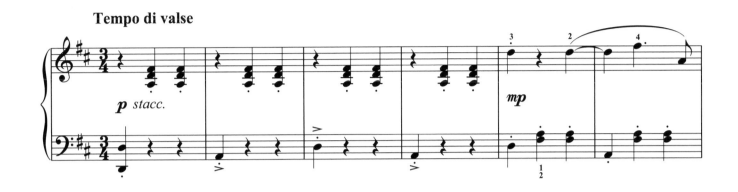

When I Am Laid In Earth

(from 'Dido And Aeneas')

Composed by Henry Purcell

Arranged by Quentin Thomas

123456789